LINE BY LINE

AN ANTHOLOGY OF
CONTEMPORARY CANADIAN POETS
WITH DRAWINGS BY HEATHER SPEARS

BOOKS OF DRAWINGS BY HEATHER SPEARS

LINE
BY
LINE

AN ANTHOLOGY OF
CONTEMPORARY CANADIAN POETS

EDITED BY AND
WITH DRAWINGS BY
HEATHER SPEARS

Ekstasis  Editions

National Library of Canada Cataloguing in Publication Data

Main entry under title:

Line by line

ISBN 1-896860-50-8

1. Canadian poetry (English)--21st century.*
I. Spears, Heather
PS8293.L46 2002   C811'.608   C2001-911562-8
PR9195.7.L46 2002

Published in 2002 by:
Ekstasis Editions Canada Ltd.
Box 8474, Main Postal Outlet
Victoria, B.C. V8W 3S1

Ekstasis Editions
Box 571
Banff, Alberta ToL oCo

THE CANADA COUNCIL | LE CONSEIL DES ARTS
FOR THE ARTS | DU CANADA
SINCE 1957 | DEPUIS 1957

BRITISH
COLUMBIA
ARTS COUNCIL
Supported by the Province of British Columbia

Line by Line: An Anthology of Contemporary Canadian Poets has been published
with the assistance of a grant from the Canada Council and the Cultural Services
Branch of British Columbia.

Printed in Canada

CONTENTS

INTRODUCTION

Drawing Canadian poets in performance has always been my particular pleasure. It's different from making a formal portrait — the poet is there but not static — involved and moving with the poem in personal, intimate ways I can hone in on if I pay close enough attention. It is a special way of listening.

I'd like to thank all the poets who generously contributed poems to go with my (not always flattering) drawings. What I asked was that the poem be "generally about line" and the submissions — some formerly published, some new and written especially for this collection — range widely; but all in some way add to the exploration of that mystery of what is line — verbal, tactile or 'visionary.' Because line to me is of almost divine significance.

Heather Spears, Copenhagen, Denmark
November, 2001

Note: *The original drawings, apart from a few purchased by the poets, are in the collection of the artist and will later be archived at the University of British Columbia.*

Some days poems lie deep
and will not rise to the lure
no matter the artful cast
and the skill of retrieve,
no matter that we hold
our breath and will
the sudden rush of poem to line.

from *poem fishing* by Glen Sorestad

LINE BY LINE

DRAWINGS BY

HEATHER SPEARS

The Line, As in Poetry: Three Variations

i)

The line is a white thread,
or so we're told. You fasten
one end of it to a tree or bed
or threshold, and footfall
by footfall, you unscroll
this line behind you

as you step into the cove to meet
whatever wants you dead,
or vice versa—

the ill will of the universe,
a shucked lover,
the core
of your own head—
compacted fire,
monstrous, horned, sacred.

You hold your breath,
one heartbite
after another.
Tastes familiar.

ii)

The line is a lifeline,
it leads you out again
to the profane. To vegetables
and sex, and eggs
and bacon. Fodder. Wallow. Time
as generally understood.
Breakfast, lunch, dinner,
architecture,
all those things
that won't miss you
when you're elsewhere.
There. Feel better?

iii)

Reverse the field and the line is black,
the cavern a whiteout.
A blank, a snow.
The monster not burning coal
but ice-furred shadow.

Where does that get you?
Out of the body, onto the page,
the line the net
in which you tangle God—
O paper wendigo—

in the midst of his blizzard,
in the midst of the avalanche
of *nihilo*,
going about his business,
wringing stars out of zero.

You haul him in,
you write him down, the Word
made word. You've earthed him,
his acts
and sufferings. He seeps
out of your fingers, your wine-dark blood
at large. You've let him out, he's gone
with the wind, he's roaring
from the mountain top:
Yum! Yum! Yum! Yum!
Now we'll have massacres.

What a bad story!
Keep your hands to yourself
next time. Don't touch that paper!
We don't need no history
around here. Leave those dead babies be!

You look what you done,
you and your gol-darn line.
You just can't leave it alone.

Phone Lines

Voicelessness—

and then, circumspectly
there are too many

inside the head and
out, sound
bytes spliced into this *a capella*

choir, each one of us
a soloist who just

had to call in, desires
inharmonic

and randomly
arranged
ad hominem, voices

multiplying
dividing

like cells whenever
receivers all
through

the night are put down
gently or picked

up and cradled
dial

tones at last   broken
or not; the dark's

dimension
less silence a gap—*agapé*—(this

brotherly love) yours

one more voice in the night
its wilderness

sped

by Telus Mobility deep
into the body
through

the ear in

to the anonymous orbit of
another's distant
desire
the body your voice is: skin

bruised by touch

tone numbers unfelt
fingers
depress, cyphers each one

of us, not so
sweet the zeros

sad solitude makes us

give voice to, leaving
the data
trace our bodyscapes come

quickly to be known by
all switches

in the receptor

brain

thrown and synaesthetic—hair
suddenly *hazel*, eyes
ebony-hard
the lip's quicksilver remoteness

licorice, quince, radicchio—

self-reflexive arias unsated
by the heat
scored
profanely into the heart by an

other

's—(*my/your*)—degraded circuitry, phone
lines
connecting to

only disconnect—

all voices safely erased.

STEPHEN MICHAEL BERZENSKY
Notes on Mandelstam

1.

Anything can be poured into a poem
        as long as it smells of life
          or reeks of death or stares down
like the cold half moon

2.

Pack all you know into the fewest lines
          the only baggage you're allowed
       to take with you
into exile, into darkness

3.

truth
is dangerous
      poems
      are dangerous
         you can
         die for poetry

whats in a name

what abt a prson
who cant heer 'd's
whn theyr th beginning
uv a word

sumwun sz   god is ded
2 them n they heer god
is ed   n thn yu introduse
sumwun 2 them say ths
is ed

n they go pleez 4 give me or
hows yr son n he has no
childrn   or his son was killd
tragikalee in a drive by shoot
ing   or a home invaysyun

or he was caut in his
studio   up all nite   working
on his nu book   th gradual
arrival uv th line in space

sum terribul msundrstanding
had takn hold uv the narrativ
elementz uv his life resulting
in a deep gash in his hed

n as he entrs thru th last veil
from heer n suddnlee undrstands
sew much abt our specees n our
places in th galaxee   his bodee

succumbing 2 infinit mattr seez
such a briteness he moovs tords
sighs   o my ed

21

at waterline

setting sun ridgepole
of this long river house

clouds the highest
branches and leaves of trees

empty shell and stones
remind of lives lived and spent

voices of travellers heard long
out of mist before their arrival

tobacco on the water:
pray for the follies of this life

thanks for being born here
for love and this journey

fire ember glow slipping
behind fingers of cloud

another dash of birds
a muskrat swimming upstream

kayaks dip their wings
coming to land for night

cherry dotted *i*
on blue inkwash

George Bowering

The lovely lines of war

the angry spaces of peace—

I am of two minds

Clinging to corpus callosum

the poet's lifeline

MARILYN BOWERING

from Letter to Janey

My singing teacher says that you have to catch the line:
the song is already in progress and you ease on board with your voice.
You never start the song yourself: its been travelling in your direction
since the beginning of time. She doesn't talk about endings,
but I believe the song continues after you stop.
You slide off, everyone listening follows you,
and you stand there together a moment on the sidelines
watching the song as it passes from hearing.

You can think of it as a train,
or an animal running because that is what it is born to do.
That's how I think of you, Janey—you're moving quickly towards
me and away—
for no particular reason.

You're simply there, in one moment,
a small dark girl in trousers and a red cotton shirt,
lifting your arms to greet me. "Come on!" you said. "Let's go see."
You said nothing could make you afraid.

I've put an ad in the paper and I hope I will find you.
But I know you might be dead.

crossing

vol...
like a
in the
den...

Colin
Larberry

...g the ...p
S A M...

26 05 99

Reading the Stream, 5AM

for Darryl Carlyle

All I saw was the play of transience
unreel before my half-awakened eyes,
listening, in a hammock slung between trees,
to the sweet time rivering in the leaves.

From that perch I watch you cast and recast
into the green flux of Cerro Pietro:
stock-still, heron-eyed, in your element
by the sparkling plash and thrum, detached now

from all but the tensed fishing line and lure
as you reel in a speckled trout to roast
between flames... Novice to initiate,

I felt like *Fionn,* poet-soon-to-be-seer,
who, left to turn the spitted Salmon, burnt
his thumb, and so was first to eat of it.

I wonder if
never sit ag

Walker 26.05.94

The Face in the Mirror

The entire house dark
save the bathroom light;
he stands in the bathysphere
and looks out;
in the mirror world
this is looking in.

At first
a glazed face
a face of glass
then textures come into focus:

lumpy plaster, pale as flesh,
the badly mixed clay,
a nose that is undescribable
as two eyes with a vacant look
turn accusing.

Then a merciful fade out
to glass again.
two eyes, a nose, a mouth;
once a popular design.

MARK COCHRANE

Poetics

This stanza is gendered feminine if the line breaks
after the word breaks.
This stanza is gendered masculine if the line breaks aft
/er the word breaks.
This stanza is E-shaped prose if the line does not break.

FRED COGSWELL

Circular Saws

When the circular saw
chewed up my fingernail
I said to myself
"This is a bad dream
and I shall wake up,"
but I didn't
and in
a few minutes
the pain began

after that I had
a scar to remind me
not to go near
circular saws

But I soon found
they had ways
of distinguishing themselves
so that watch as I might
they were always
hurting me

now inside and out
I am covered with scars
but that is not
the worst I've learned
the worst thing is
that under the masks
I wear and without
intending to be
I am a circular saw

CHRISTOPHER DEWDNEY
Fovea Centralis

A man is looking out of his eyes and is reading or talking. He gesticulates "expressively" while he talks, or his comment pencil glitters in the electric light. The frequency of his nervous movements becomes continuous, is hands begin to occupy space through movement. The solid form that is inhabited by his hands pulsates, forms a ring, a tunnel around his vision. The solid is composed of movement and is dangerous, his eyes wander, verging on sleep or hypnosis.

LOUIS DUDEK

The Dust of Ninevah

Take a handful of the dust of Ninevah.
In this dust are the once powerful, the rich,
   the starving poor;
the athletes and the invalids, the successful and
   the unsuccessful;
the gifted and the ungifted, the kings and the beggars:
all are here, mixed in this dust.

They are forgotten, and nobody knows their names.

In a few thousand years we too will be like these people.
We too will be forgotten, and lie buried in the dust of time.

Margaret Dyment

Hatch 20 June 86

MARGARET SLAVIN DYMENT

Tracing a Line

burned my bridges
line of fire across the sky
from Ottawa to Calgary
then embers at dark mountains
night
no way to return

this morning is grey
my violet survived the trip
bruised. we go to meet the
cat, stoned but OK
daughter not phoning
daughter out there somewhere
friends
new starts

I remember my father's death
how I learned to trace
a line through what yet lives
memory, letters, already one call
my man shaving in the next room
violet, daughter, friend
little stoned angry cat
my own heart.

a thin line

the couple in the next apartment learning how to fit together their
skins thin as these walls   thin as new ice   the sounds they make
like the sounds new ice makes when its skin hardens gathering cold
full of

my hand around this pencil like a knife   somethings's got to give: all
this taken as given   the couple in the next apartment their skins
making brittle music   thin entering   slippery slope   the safest place
in the belly of a whale

through the window: a ghost sea   white birches haunt the fog

inside, each word I draw is a red herring   apostrophes for eyes
a leaf for a skeleton   as if they could belong to light   swim
through space
        as

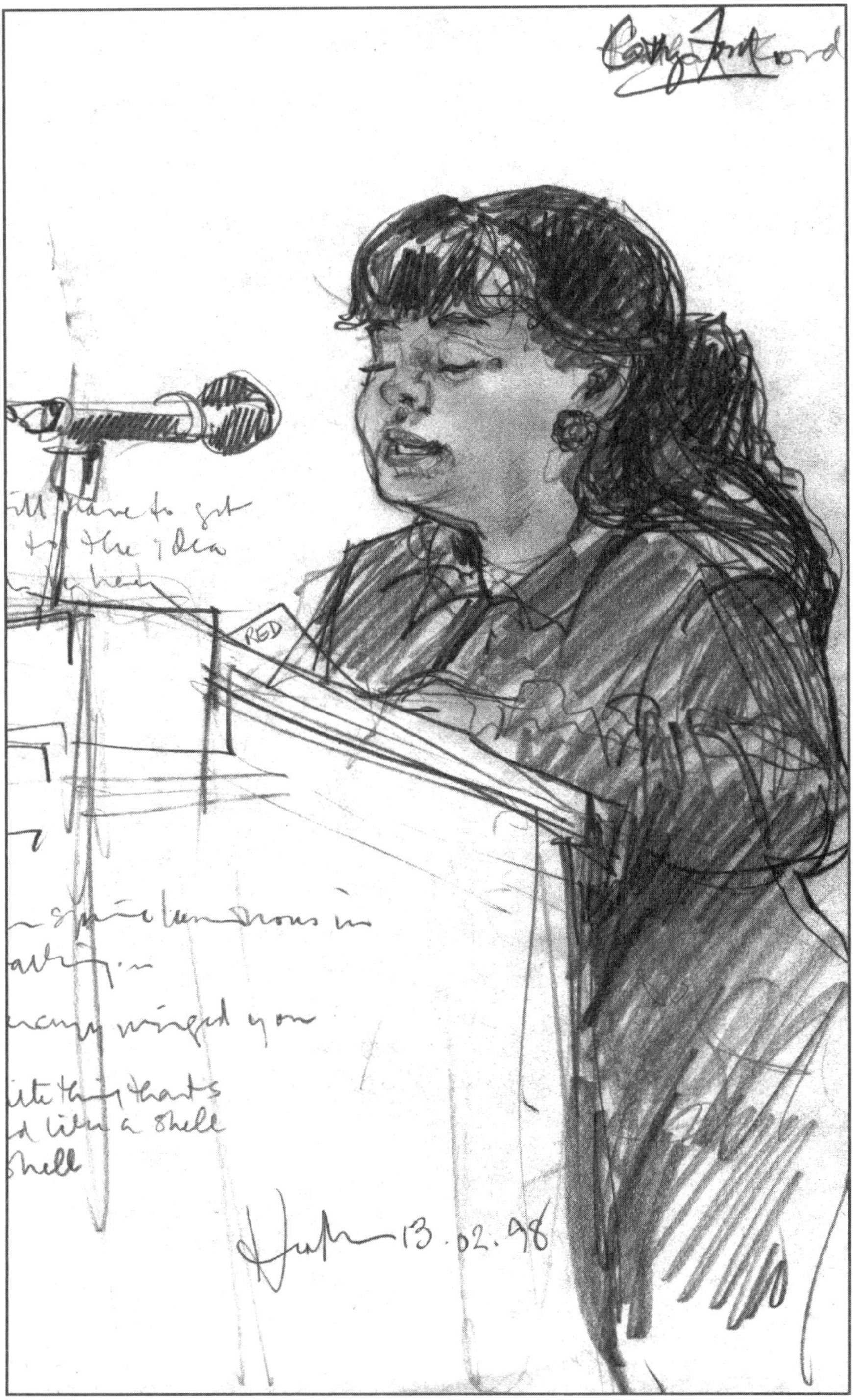
RED
13.02.98

The Black Pansy is Called Black Pansy

When the century moves, *on* from the angel of death
a bookmark collection of blue eyes, *like butterflies*
in perfectly organized specimen drawers

the man who played the piano and
        broadcast it over the camps
at night

a kindly continuous terrorization of the minds whose bodies he trusted
to give up their inadvertent secrets, the shading of light
tell the truth, these were not secret anyone was keeping

women and children first, *let us not forget,*
the vivisection of hope, humanity, killed people

real people, children
the children whose eyes he tried to change the colour of

remember, you were born just after this all stopped mid-way
the afflicitions at a pause, mere gradations of shadow

        born, with pansy black eyes, so black your eyes were purple

just keep the politics out of your poetry, your creative non-fiction

the century will still turn
        its graveyards full, its winds scattered with ash

finally peaceful, the women and children injected first, three times a week
like butterflies pinned at the spine, poison, feces, formaldehyde

still, the century will turn
above all, do not mention his name

        and never your own

Drawing the Line

Voices, data, artefacts, when what I want
is the lean dirge of departure. The last
sound from the doubtful ship, a shrill

keening that moves like fog across the sea
and up the tarred pilings of the pier
into your bones. As if song could sustain

us, fill the void, stitch elegance into rags.
Left behind to please a childless uncle,
siblings in steerage. The stark profile

in the second-class porthole, as the blunt
bow of the steamer inches past in reverse,
resembled a cameo. What the heart

knows: files, restricted documents.
Fake brick siding on the shed out back
where blood flowed from the torn string

of a boy's foreskin. A crude fridge that wore
its coiled brain on top for all the world to see.
Rain pisses down, westerlies drive cumulus

up the inlet. Mountains in the distance
change colour, green to light-blue, until
indistinguishable from pale sky. Old

blood-pump, its mythic inheritance, worn
on the sleeve, corded and hanging
like a curse or amulet. I tried to sketch

the Abbey ruins, temples the Duncombes
constructed at Rivieaulx. Neoclassical,
as out of place as they were of scale.

I'm not Wordsworth, I have no patience
with second-hand sublimity. Margaret
gives me a gauge carved by my grandfather,

used to inscribe a cutting-line on planks
of a house I'll never set foot in. My fingers
brush the threaded shank, the interlocking

nuts of the scriber. Its sharpened point
penetrates the callous of my thumb.
Demarcations, all the lines that join us.

A Jar of Light

You reach for a handful of the city,
those sparklers stop buildings;
sheen of elegance, women
their men stepping always behind them.
The few slices of the moon
that locust flowers are
looped over your fingers like silk cords.

Reaching with that extended arm
forward and back, bringing in the light
of everyone you've ever known,
none of them are there tonight.

The past steps out of its shadows
trying on your old shoes.   Some garish,
others with miraculous and ordinary dust.

The light trapped in your fist
smelling slightly of pickles
like that jar with its jagged holes
the day you filled it
with the darkness of bees.

Frantic against the glass, upside down
as close as they can to the holes,
their furred feet worrying what little air.
The lid loosened,
the droning terror follows you.

After supper the jar tilted
with the stale lilac and green label.
You wait by the bushes for fireflies,
and fill it again.

And on the hill with your jar of light,
that tomorrow will be gone,
the glass bottom spotted
with the bodies of light.

You release them,
their lights disperse.
This time you do not run,
no longer afraid.

The city jumps in your fist
as grasshoppers did,
a tiny mouth gaping and sucking air,
its body livid in your grip.
You love and fear it at once.

Your fingers caught
between the tension of powerful legs
and the wise reflex of your hands.
Its green face before you,
released, high leaping into the green waves.

Moon

What she said when she pointed to the birthmark on Lisa's face
was *moon*. 478 days old and the fields of her language overlap
below the eye, above the corner of her mother's mouth. The child sees
the line begins in the arm. From our faces she knows eye, teeth, nose;
from books she knows moon, sheep, lion, and then this which no
one taught, though it is no less miraculous than looking at a yellow
disc on a blue page and saying *moon*, than pointing to a gibbous glow
and saying *moon*. And yet the tiny dark moon pulls the tide of the eye
towards itself again as Lisa speaks of this single syllable at the tip
of her baby's finger.
Everyone I tell this story to as the story of Emma's First Poem
agrees though still I doubt the claim to first, my baby authoring all
this time without intent, guiding the reader the way she takes my hand
when we walk. From the birth to the syllable to the line, she is
talking about us, and every day we are more like parents, inside
the words.

LALA HEINE-KOEHN

Poems for my Lovers

I have written many poems for you
my lovers
what I did not dare to say I wrote
between the lines
the space has become too narrow
now I must write
a line   upon a line

Jodsoll

our faas tu
in the sexua

No one had
katten
The Book of Sl

Huth 27.05.9

Me, Mom and the Moulin Rouge

My mother dragged pubescent me
Across Europe to expose me to history and art
For so many weeks even Reubens' women made me drool.
My pornographic memory took only quick smiles from girls
Before the leash of culture yanked me away.
Our day in Paris was the day the Louvre was closed.
Instead we went to the second home
Of Degas and Lautrec—the Moulin Rouge
Where dancers once posed long enough
To become beautiful canvas blurs. So there we were
Right up front, me leaving my glasses at the hotel,
Tired of having to see what was good for me.
So I never saw the topless chorus line except
As flesh tone fuzz with swaying motions,
And I never saw my mother's face decompose
Into its basic geometry, a pained facade
She held all evening, smiling (even during
The on-stage dolphin act's final trick—
The nuzzling free of the trainer's bikini top).
Not wanting to be caught squinting, I watched
Through an impressionist haze what she saw too clearly.
She could never again view the paintings of dancers
Without the background shadows becoming leering artists.
I guess you could say we both got what we were
Looking for in Europe, although when you travel
Crossed lines always mix up your wishes
With someone else's wants.

DG Jones

The
somewhere
dog

D.G. JONES

Likeness, or "A Woman Smiling"

so from chaos we abstract
recursive symmetries

changeful

yet of flower or beetle or the wind, familar
as a mackerel sky

the simple fold between the eyes
cartoonists catch
as "doubt," as "concentration," as the "stress"
beauty submits to
being human

simplify, but yet suggest
the line before the smile
                       and after
that parentheses

For Gerri

These lines jump from the tips of my stiff fingers
to explore the circled universe of memory.
They follow the outlines of distant mountains,
the edges of leaves in the sunlight, the jagged
fractures of crystalline thought. They snap
to the vague silhouette of the horizon
as it recedes from your grasp. They follow
the troubled routes of angels who dispense
wispy messages of hope to the afflicted, appearing
in the evening sky as luminous vapour trails
dispersing gradually like clouds of spent desire.
At daybreak these nebulous lines gather again
to illuminate the edge of a coastline that grows
longer as you measure it. They are the weft
of history flying through the warp of time
as every living thing renews itself
in the next generation. These threads
are straws in the biblical mortar, grass
in the swallows' nest under the eaves, mossy
paths that lead from here to then, thin
precarious wires strung through the forest
between now and there.

And when this circuitry is complete,
when each point on the grid is joined
to its corresponding opposite number,
when the last ones and zeroes have fallen into place,
and the unobtrusive hum of background radiation
moves into prominence as a slow symphony
of cosmic bliss, these tangles of intent
will resolve quietly into simple links
of love. And on that designated night
when the north wind moans, and a gnarled
cedar branch rubs against the thin pane
of your bedroom window, these lines will merge
with the intricate map of your moist palm.

Reflections on Line

When you write, you lay out a line of words. Annie Dillard

***

Drop me a line you said
without elaboration.
Here I sit, uncertain.
You did not say how long
from where
and to what end.

I will *lay out a line of words*
hand-picked for truth
and clarity. Will you wait for them?
They will be brief
as breath, true as the morning light
and dangerous.

***

You have drawn a line on sand.
How will you prevent the inevitable
drifting in? Try as you will you can not
stop me from staring across
to where that field of blue flax shines,
a morning diamond. Shines like water
under the June sun. What you have made
the wind will blow away, the pounding rain in one short night
obliterate. Even now
that elegant bird
preening its emerald feathers
is preparing to fly over, singing.

***

Here on the prairie
line is the unattainable
horizon, the white winding highway
a thin ribbon, a finger pointing
waveringly toward it.

I will come to you straight
as the crow flies
making a beeline.

***

Consider the fine line that separates
theory and practice
light and the noon shadow
You from me

Divest yourself of fear if you can,
and consider the absolute
line that hovers thread-like between
silence and breath.

The Sealing

This is for your eyes alone. I have
folded the paper precisely, one third and then another,
and placed the parchment into its envelope. Here
I place my seal. I heat the honeyed wax and watch it
drip by drip until it forms a liquid pool on the seal
and then I take my hand and make it into a fist
and, standing, press my whole body down
until my house is made there, my seal, my isignia,
my mark, my making. These are my words.
They say: *This is for you.*
Your hands, your eyes, your body.
You are the one I have made
this for, in the quiet of my room,
in the dead of night, one word and then another,
and now no one can break it but you.

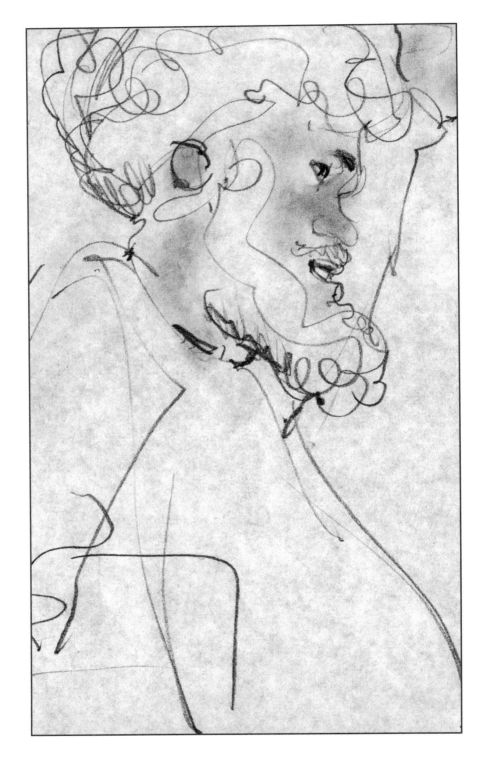

CHRISTOPHER LEVENSON

Intersections

From the Blue Ridge lookout you can see
far down the valley the Interstate snaking through
stands of old pine: somehow
that road completes our Eden.

Always the curve cutting across
harsh grids: twigs lashing the pane,
the swallow's neat adobe rounding out
raw concrete pillar and strut, a bellying sail
flapping against the mast.
So soft converges with rigid,
shaping androgyny.

The Fisherman

The world was first a private park
Until the angel, after dark,
Scattered afar to wests and easts
The lovers and the friendly beasts.

And later still a home-made boat
Contained Creation set afloat,
No rift nor leak that might betray
The creatures to a hostile day.

But now beside the midnight lake
One single fisher sits awake
And casts and fights and hauls to land
A myriad forms upon the sand.

Old Adam on the naming-day
Blessed each and let it slip away:
The fisher of the fallen mind
Sees no occasion to be kind,

But on his catch proceeds to sup;
Then bends, and at one slurp sucks up
The lake and all that therein is
To slake that hungry gut of his,

Then whistling makes for home and bed
As the last morning breaks in red;
But God the Lord with patient grin
Lets down his hook and hoicks him in.

Courage/ Cour de rage

for my mother, Betty Page

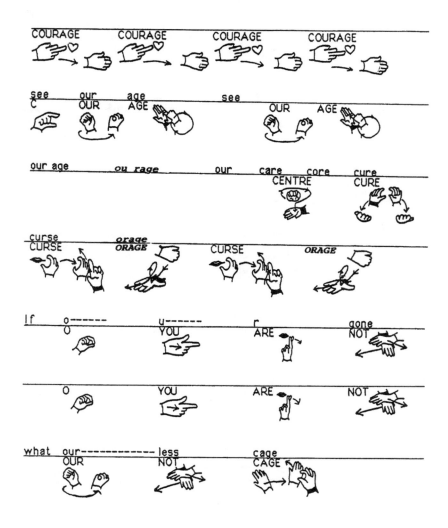

bring back "r"
ARE

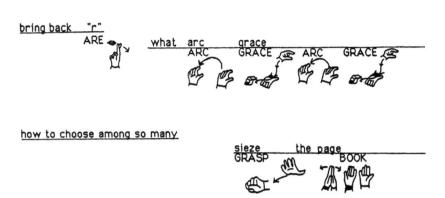

what arc grace
ARC GRACE ARC GRACE

how to choose among so many

sieze the page
GRASP BOOK

all lines are self-limned

courage heart's rage
COURAGE HEART RAGE

74

The Line

This is not the poem, this line
I'm feeding you. And the thought
that this line is not the poem
is not it either. Instead
the thought of what this line is
not is the weight that sinks it
in. And though this image of
that thought as a weight is quite
a neat figure of speech, you
know what it's not—though it did
this time let the line smoothly
arc to this spot, and now lets
it reach down to one other,
one further rhyme—the music
of which almost does measure
up, the way it keeps the line
stirring through the dampening
air. Oh, you know you can hear
the lure in that. As you know
you've known from the start the self
referring this line's doing
was a hook—a sharp, twisted
bit of wit that made you look
and see how clear it is no
part of this line or its gear
could be the poem. Still it cast
and kept the line reeling out
till now at last the hook's on
to itself and about to
tie this line I'm feeding you
up with a knot. Referring
to itself has got the line
and us nowhere. So clever's
not what the poem is about

either. We're left hanging there
while something like a snout starts
nudging at your ear, nibbling
near my mouth—and it's likely
it's the poem about to take
the bait. From the inside ought
to be a great way to learn
what the poem is. And we'll use
this line when the poem's drawn it
taut and fine as breath to tell
what we know, where we are and
where we'll go—unless the line
breaks. How would it feel, knowing,
at last, what the poem really
is, to lack the line to speak?

www.cyberus.ca/~cmo
The poem as a
machine made of words

Colin Morton

Earth Bed

Less fiercely than river
carves banks

more subtly than glacier
hollows lake

you fit my body
to yours even now

as you turn in sleep
this stone to breathing soil

ROGER NASH

A Long Line at the Horizon

Ships tow aromatic islands endlessly by, laden with camomile, basil, hyssop and bird-shit.

The Poems of Octavio Paz

Sunlight on stone.
The poems of Octavio Paz.
Light in moonlight. The transparency of water.
A wave cutting through the night.
The poems of Octavio Paz. A book open
on a beach whose pages are blank
whose lines are silent
waiting for the voice
of the poet to give them
shape.
Clarity of the air. The visitation of
a hummingbird at a blossom
fed on the nectar of the moment.
A stone in sun. The moment's moment.
A wave that falls in love
with a man, a man swimming in love.
Poetry invents the invisible:
time and truth cast a shadow
and the shadow of that shadow
is poetry.
A printing press beating without cessation
the poems of Octavio Paz
cast into hot type.
Looking out along the line of ocean against sky
the green islands are the breasts
of sleeping women resting in the bath.
Air above.
Water below.
Moon at night. Moon hollow in the sea.
Silent world. A breath in the stillness.
The poems of Octavio Paz.

Training

The train a short sentence
  not of thought
    stammers a long line over white snow pages
like some unlovely gray ship
  it tears between standing wave drifts
    only the moon measures, opens
a bow wave in the closing sea
  of perspective
but sight tows a zipper that shuts
the gap of where we were.

Inside, a child wakes: the train
  with its jumping seats and important noises
    is still absurdly in the same place he is:
a narrow nightfogged city
  much like the city he left in
    that other today before sleep. Awake
he sits still in his swaying seat.

Crossings understand the train.
They wave arms cluck lights bell the night
  & cut the traffic that isn't there
    in deference to the scar the train
stitches over mooning white drifts.

The train's in a hurry to join city to
  city since perspective is nip-
    ping at its tail (smaller)
      when longer) so it
        stammers the same
          line to the
            listening
              land

Motor Trip

A splendid headful

spools of rolling land
fenced and unfolding

endless thought of you
a drawn red line across the greenscape   all
mywhere paralleling

and

descending and ascending
silver hoops
glancing and entering
in flights of larks

Senex

An old man getting out of the bathtub
    Hears his grandchildren skipping
        Outside.
Caught in the mirror over the washbasin
    Could that aging satyr
      With dangling genitals
    Wrinkled and sagging,
One day with an erect wand have produced
    Those shrieks, that glitter
        Under the shade of the satalpa trees
        On his back lawn?
Could this lonely limp fish, a mere sprat,
    And those two crusts of scrotal dough,
Have fed thousands of the hungriest?
    The answer, apparently,
      Is
      "Yes!"

Water

This is not one of the Sefiroi
that is burning, phosphorescent,
in this dark room—the shape
of the night is showing
through the form of the room—
but the scent that wafts from it
is the scent of hay:
it is a thing of light,
a nest for birds, a jug
that will hold no water:
it is the body.

Mountains and trees are also
thin filaments of light:
the mind, perfectly attuned,
will look through them
and see Nothing—they are
the heavy seedheads of grass
in rain;

as soon as the body steps
out of the door
and the wind moulds itself
exactly to its face, it ceases
to be the body,
but is the threshing floor;

music is continually fighting
to return to its first
note, but no longer has within it
the form of a tree—it can form
the song of a tree, but can put forth no leaves,
gently fingering the light
like angels.

I have just stepped out the back door
into the sky. The light
in the leaves under the apricot trees,
and the light off the water
on those leaves, to hold
the frost from the roots,
is reflecting the sky:
the sun is burning within them—
but cooled, and still.

If you break apart
the sacred geometry of the Sefiroi,
you get no more than a heap
of light on the ground,
that quickly seeps out through the grass
until it is a skin
that so perfectly fits the shape
of leaf-blade and gravel
that it has unlearnt
itself—and all so quickly
that the mind does not see
that it is there, or even
that it was within its hands.

With such visions the body
walks down out of the bush,
dark with rain, smelling of clouds, and simply
to see the light burn up over its face
and to feel the shadows of light
burn down its throat as the door opens,
knocks lightly on the door of the mind
and asks for water. Music too
tends to unlearn itself
when thrown into the grass.

The body sees all, and because
it does not know what to make of it,
and with what it knows
cannot return into the water
the mind has given it
in a white pitcher,
but can drink it,
and so, bitterly, drinks—rain,
and wind through alders, the moon
shivering, a blur—and so
shivers, it dreams;
and those dreams are the mind.

If you break apart
the sacred geometry
of the mind, you get the body:
it smells faintly of a flame.
You can learn much from it,
like water poured down the throat
out of the hands,
directly into the rough wood-wind
notes of a tree,
so coarse they seem at first
without relation to water.

Labels

The baby
just born into this
world has been greeted
and well taken care of.
Already a variety of
labels have been
etched on him.
One for race.
One for colour. One
for religion and maybe
one for a caste.
At the same time he
is told
you are born into a free world—
Congratulations!

The baby smiles and
accepts every thing in
good faith.

One day when he grows
into a boy and the boy
into man it will suddenly
dawn on him;
 no body knows him
 only his labels.

Shaping

trapped by my shaping
the impingement of form
upon my self &

      outside

                the world
surrounds me like a line
defines me   my shape
compresses me
the expanse of my body anchors me
grounds me in the world
my voice is strangled & disguised
when I scream
the sound crashes against my form
ricochets back
stunsmebruisesmekeepsme
captive
           deep
within my skin

The Saning

It might be one of those mornings
when the city is no longer a miracle.
You would be running through the woods,
concentrating on your breathing,
when its little hand reaches up
from a pile of leaves
and grabs your ankle.

This is the saning.
It is there for you to discover;
dirt in its eyes,
its umbilical cord uncut.

You are alone in the forest
with the ghosts of your ancestors
and an inarticulate child.
You have fallen into
one of the holes in the fire,
but you know what to do
because you have eaten kangaroo meat
and dreamed of a moment like this

You've been running for years
and your hair has turned white,
but you still have what you need;
your mother's sewing scissors
engraved with roses, and a red
washcloth that won't show the blood.

You pick it up in your arms.
You cut the cord with the scissors
and clean its eyes and its mouth,
then you breathe into it.
This is the moment you get to
invent your own religon.

The poem becomes bigger than you.
It is filled with your breath.
It makes you remember yourself
as a child, standing in front of a door.
You have been bathed and powdered
and you want to leave because
you have fallen in love with your own
footprints in the sweet smelling dust.

This is what you are following
now, when the poem goes to the light.
You watch it walk away.
Perhaps it will turn to thank you.

STEPHEN SCOBIE

Dear Heather,

What can I say about the line? The line
returns, always, to its starting point: it is
a question of margins, marginality,
where the line ends
it begins. It comes back like a ghost
haunting our breath. It dies a long death
on its search for the right hand margin
and then is born again. Revenant, Resurrectionist—
the line is all we have
we have to live by. Our lives on the line.

But is that what you meant? The poetic line?
or that primal mark, hand to paper
(sand, canvas, wall, stone: blank surface)
first gesture of inscription
already dividing space, giving gesture and ground,
line of a face in profile, line
of trees on a distant horizon?

We walk the line, we draw the line,
sometimes we cross the line. It is a sign
(a lyin' sign) for limit and transgression.
"Oh you see that line that's movin' through the station"—
we line 'em up and shoot 'em down.
The line starts here.

Heather, my favourite line is the coast:
long stutter of islands and inlets
and on a particular beach, a shifting line
moving to some
equation: where the tide
advances and returns
across the level slip of sand.

101

I want a line as slow as that, twice-daily pulse,
or the breath-line pausing, reaching out
and coming home. Dear sweet familiar ghost
on the margin once again.

Stephen

JOE ROSENBLATT

My life is dancing on a hook

I glitter in the freezing depths
where Fate has set me up for bait
to tantalize the eyes of devils
inside the belly of this grave.

Secured to a deep fishing line
above the seabed of the night
my life is dancing on a hook
delighting squid, bottomfish
and wily crabs who do a jig.

In praise of a gyrating visitor
the bubbling mob illumes its love.
They mouth an effervescent blessing
and I perceive their amorous prayers

before my flesh is kissed away.

JAY RUZESKY

Lines Under Water

You cast from shore and the lure
disturbs an image of you and of pines and mountains.
Water swallows the line and you are drawn
down into that green place by thread that
disappears through a mirror.

In dark rooms
you sink past your mother, father,
houses you once lived in—drift
down gently like a leaf
falling through warm air you
look up through a lead glass shimmer.

On the other side is real life, but this,
this is a place where your thoughts
are fractured logs and gangly weeds;
your mind rests
in the dream of what it already knows.

Writing swims under the surface,
each rising bubble a word wanting out.

This is where you pitch a line between
language and recall, wrestling with
the forgotten world that snags
on your barbed, your searching hooks.

Aphelion

My father loves with the knuckles
of his words, dottled fists
that cut the air, find
an attenuated target.

On what might be his deathbed
he tries again to force the line
and fails, for once, to complete
the bony kiss.

Such effort sends a weary man,
however resolute,
          tilting into his age,
to go on tilting,
long after I've abandoned him
to himself.

poem fishing

It is the right weather for poems:
gentle drizzle spins the morning grey
and no sunglints will strike
the monofilament we cast
across chill water.

Some days poems lie deep
and will not rise to the lure
no matter the artful cast
and skill of retrieve,
no matter that we hold
our breath and will
the sudden rush of poem to line.

Today I am archetypal fisherman,
intent on the moment, alert
to signals from below the surface.
The rod bends, a poem has taken hold.

The teaching of drawing

a line is
nothing
it is the turning away of a stone, a shoulder
it is the terrified awareness of absence
faltering into consciousness and speaking itself in a whisper
it is this hair, hazardous as grass
it is the ground, your feet splay,
black earth fastens onto them.
it is the inside of your mouth
parting on darkness
or your genitals, the perfect detail of accident
it is the abstract of the world
it is the slow recording
of what happens between my eye
and the skin of your neck
averting and tightening
over aeons
it is the gunshot stammer
of flames in bracken
it is the track of an insect
dragging itself painfully by millimetres
across the surface of the cortex
or a yell of pain
finished instantly—
silence of it.
scar of it.

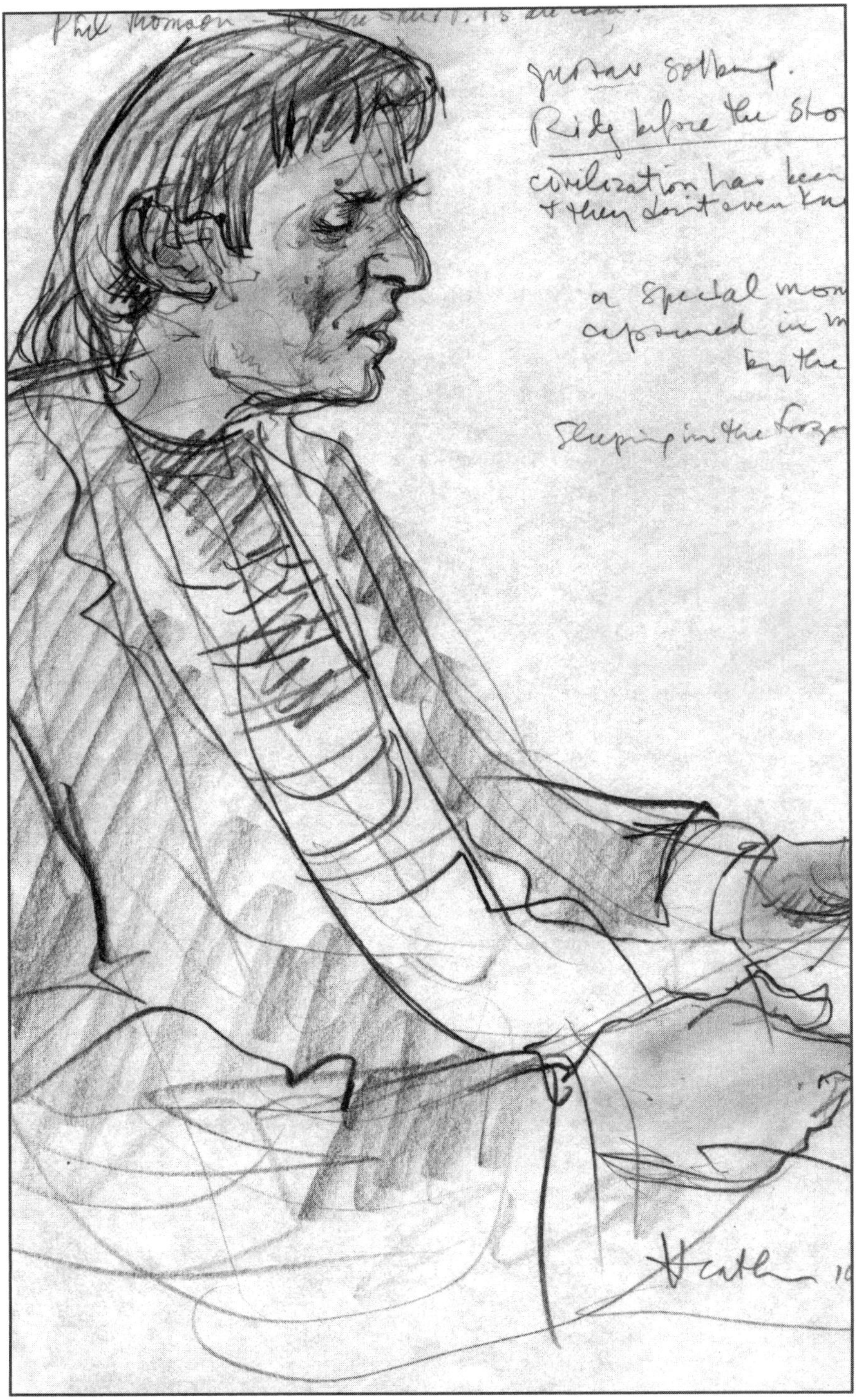

Brown Clipboard Poem

This poem is a brown clipboard
angled across the surface
of a green painted door desk
scratched and worn
with faded graffiti
a metal clamp
white loose leaf paper
blue parallel lines
three holes on the left
a faintly red margin line
masking tape repair

Black cylindrical plastic instrument
with felt tip
first formed these words
guided by the eye and hand
of a writer

Before this happened
the brown clipboard was a poem.

Hockey Poem

Poems are something
like hockey players
nurtured in the junior leagues
the farm teams of the subconscious

Every so often
you advance them to the majors
hoping
they'll make the grade for you
score literary goals
deke the critics
When they don't come up to snuff
you ship them
back down to the minors

Always
you draw more culls than champions
sometimes useful workhorses
who can't skate
sometimes dazzling skaters
who can't score
Gingerly
you juggle your lines
assemble your teams
All too often
they don't even make the playoffs

But a poet
is like a patient coach
The game
must go on
After every defeat
you lick your wounds
study the mental draft choices
always on the lookout
for a Gretsky.

like waiting in line

Waiting is fixed, the other side of waiting is free.
Leonard Cohen, 1995

like waiting in line for a movie
you've wanted to see for months
outside the theatre you're so close to it
you gaze at the poster, try to remember
the trailer, smell the popcorn
flip through last week's *Georgia Straight*

the people who come out of the early showing walk by
arrogantly (so it seems when you're waiting)
because they're beyond waiting, they've seen it
and they're free—they gave themselves up to it
and have been given themselves back, free

haven't you ever wanted to just wrestle one of them
to the ground and scream is it worth it
tell me—should I maybe just leave now?

but no matter what one of those jokers says
you've got to stay, whatever weather
because this is a vigil now
and you've got to see it through
for yourself, for everyone who's ever waited

in the movie line take the hand
of the person in front of and behind you
wait there expectantly, not just for your movie
but for everyone, wait for everyone
who ever waited glassy-eyed and nauseous
        for movies change cheques benefits
        toilets buses trains ferries
        journeys exiles falls arrivals
        concert tickets bad dates
        pelvic exams blood test results—

the whole confusing show
to which we give ourselves

Spring Thing

Ok. It's all right with me
   if you insist on repeating yourself
      I do that too, but the wonder

is in small change.
   I'll give you three lines
      for a new strategy to set things straight:

You were always phenomenal
   epiphenomenal—and blind.
      Open my eyes, lidded with this slow snow.

Walking Down the Staircase

He follows behind, all his mute
passions folded inside like sheet music.
Too bad summer's over, but it was beginning
to look like a rerun movie.
I roll up my sleeves and keep moving.
Out in front I hold a hand mirror—a kind of torch to light the way.
Like the sky, his face is always changing.
Beyond his reflection, our younger selves
swim in a sea of chalky blue.
If I knew the phase into which the moon has entered
I'd know why his words surprise like a bat's swoosh.
On the way down we pass huge circular windows.
Not much hangs on the walls
except black-and-white photographs.
Those and the cardboard fruit
children cut out of all the beautiful colours.
I keep thinking I'm pregnant.
If we could sit for a moment in the Penguin Cafe
I'd try to explain this overwhelming desire
to stop and make my body a home.
No one knows where these steps lead
except down
to the piano's last few bars.
His eyes are fixed on the back of my knees.
This is a good thing; it means the line of poetry
scribbled inside my jeans pocket have begun to ripen.
He of course had walked behind me
long enough to know
there is no scrawl
I would not try to decipher, and anyway
who can understand why they're walking down a staircase
in boots meant for more rugged terrain.

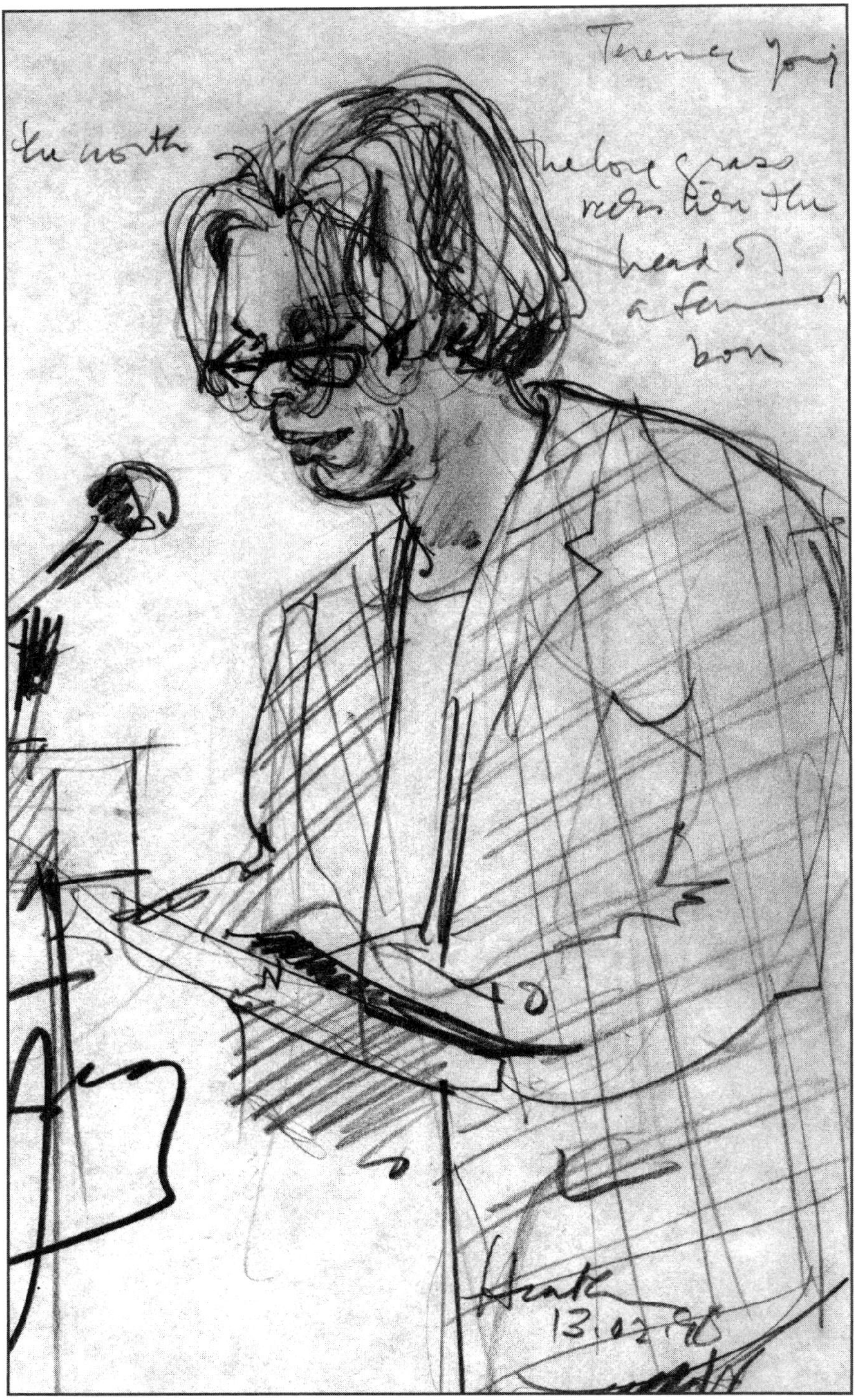

On the Juan de Fuca Trail,
Some Time in Late Spring

There is no answer when I call my son,
nothing to break the relentless surf
that rises like a wall of white noise,
inescapable as gravity, the sound track
of every west coast camper's dream.

No answer at all, just three rings
and my own voice telling me to speak after the tone.
I press the portable against my ear
like a seashell, in search of something miraculous,
a boy at home on a Saturday afternoon.

Hikers pass me on the trail. They thread by,
embarrassed to see another yuppie with a toy phone,
even here, perched above these breakers,
among ferns and giant spruce,
man-eating salal.

He should be with us
but he is all distance now,
all hands off and sleeping late, coming in at two
from a concert, a rave,
not a good word to say about anything,
not a word at all,
like someone sworn to secrecy,
silent eater, wraith who lives among us,
who closes doors behind him so quickly
you'd think a demon was biting at his heels.

I should be a real parent, force him
to come as I did when he was small,
when he had no choice: *shoes, coat,
let's go sport.* The kind of parent
who draws a line in the sand,
then dares his child to cross it.

End of the Line

Underneath the limestone cliff shaped
as much by the river as the river
is bound by the cliff, everything moves
except our survey line
clear-cut through the bush.

Like star light recorded on film,
dragonflies hover on the bark
of a chainsawed cedar.
Cedar roots grow over obstacles
no longer there, hugging themselves tight,
dead limbs keeping them apart
like the same old arguments
year after year.

Ostrich ferns wave to clouds
crossing the sun as the river returns
from olive green to gold.
Two maples thicken together at chest height,
growth rings merging, with just enough space
for three white butterflies to dance
above this oblong map of the world.

We sit at the end of lines we have drawn,
grateful they have taken us back to circle
of sky, curve of tree and river,
back where things come from, even
the gentle hum of a mosquito
searching for blood.

LIVES OF THE POETS

Margaret Atwood is the author of more than twenty-five books of poetry, fiction and non-fiction, and her work has been translated into more than thirty languages. Her newest novel, *The Blind Assassin*, was published in September, 2000 and won the Booker Prize. She lives in Toronto.

John Barton has published eight award-winning books of poetry, including *A Poor Photographer, Hidden Structure, Great Men, Notes Toward a Family Tree, Designs from the Interior, Sweet Ellipsis* and, most recently, *Hypothesis* (House of Anansi, 2001). He currently lives in Ottawa, where he co-edits *Arc: Canada's National Poetry Magazine*.

Steven Michael Berzensky (also known as Mick Burrs) is the author of six books of poetry and 24 chapbooks. His latest collection is *The Names Leave the Stones: Poems New & Selected* (Coteau Books, 2001). A former editor of *Grain* literary magazine, he currently resides in Yorkton, Saskatchewan.

bill bissett is the author of over 40 books including *the last photo uv th human soul*. He has read and performed around the world. He has created a written language all his own, an embodiment of Canadian and North American idioms.

Joe Blades is a writer, artist, editor and publisher living in Fredericton. He runs *New Muse of Contempt* magazine and Broken Jaw Press/Maritimes Arts Projects Productions, and is producer/host of *Ashes, Paper & Beans* on CHSR 97.9 FM. Since 1980, his poetry has appeared in magazines, videos, art exhibitions, anthologies, chapbooks, books and on radio. Joe travels extensively, giving readings and workshops across Canada, and occasionally in the US and Scotland.

George Bowering was born in 1936 in Canada. He has published many collections of poetry, novels, short stories and literary criticism, and his selected poems appeared in 1993. He is a widely-read commentator on Canadian culture and has received many awards for poetry and fiction. One of his novels, *Caprice*, is being made into a film this year.

Marilyn Bowering was born in Winnipeg, Manitoba, and raised and educated in Victoria, BC. Her first book of poetry was published in 1973. Since then she has published a number of award winning books including *Autobiography* which received the 1997 Pat Lowther Prize for Poetry and was nominated for the Governor General's Award. *Visible Worlds,* her latest novel, received the 1998 Ethel Wilson Prize for fiction and was nominated for the 1999 Orange Prize. Her most recent book is *Human Bodies: New and Collected Poems 1987-1999*. She now makes her home with her family in Sooke, BC.

Ron Charach is a poet and practicing psychiatrist who lives in Toronto. He is the editor of *The Naked Physician: Poems about the Lives of Patients and Doctors* as well as a poetry column in *The Medical Post*. His sixth book, *Dungenessque*, was published in 2001 by Signature Editions.

Fred Cogswell began writing poems in 1932. Since then he has published original poems and translations, and was for a time the editor of *The Fiddlehead*. Even after his retirement in 1983, he has added at least one book of poetry or translation a year. The latest, *Deeper Than Mind*, will be out shortly.

Christopher Dewdney has published over ten books of poetry, including *Predators of Adoration* and *Radiant Inventory*, both of which were nominated for Governor General's Awards. A first prize winner of the CBC Literary Competition, Dewdney has also received a third Governor General's Award nomination for *The Immaculate Perception*, a non-fiction book of popular essays about consciousness, language and dreams. In 1994 McClelland and Stewart published *Demon Pond*. The *Globe and Mail* wrote that the poems in *Demon Pond* "have a haunting, stately quality: they truly suggest the 'mystery of everything' as manifested in the act of love."

A native of Montreal, **Louis Dudek** taught at McGill University from 1951 to 1984. The author of over twenty-six books and editor of numerous anthologies, he founded many of the phenomenal small presses and magazines which have helped define the very essence of Canadian literature. Poet, essayist, translator, publisher, editor, literary provocateur, he was "Canada's most important—that is to say, consequential—modern voice," wrote Robin Blaser in his Introduction to Dudek's *Infinite Worlds* (Véhicule Press). Current books include *The Caged Tiger* and *Reality Games* (Empyreal Press) as well as *The Poetry of Louis Dudek, Definitive Edition* (The Golden Dog). This important figure in Canadian literature died March, 2001.

Margaret Slavin Dyment has published a collection of fiction, *Drawing the Spaces* (Orca) and two chapbooks of poetry: *I Didn't Get Used To It* (Ouroboros), and *Tracing a Line* (Ekstasis). She is founder of the Victoria School of Writing, and in 2000-01 was writer-in-residence at Trent University, Peterborough, Ontario.

Jannie Edwards' first book of poetry is *The Possibilities of Thirst* (Rowan). She lives and writes in Edmonton where she teaches literature and composition at Grant MacEwan College. A current project is a video that features poetry translated into American Sign Language.

Cathy Ford was born in Lloydminster, Saskatchewan and grew up in northern British Columbia. She has published fifteen books, chapbooks and folios to date. She has worked for many years as a community and arts activist committed to improving the status of women, especially women artists, in Canada, and internationally. She has served as President of the League of Canadian Poets, and was editor and co-publisher at Caitlin Press for ten years. Currently she freelances as a contract editor and book designer, columnist for *The Word is Out* magazine, and creative writing workshop leader and teacher.

After teaching in Montreal for twenty years, **Gary Geddes** has returned to the west coast, where he lives at French Beach on Vancouver Island. He has written and edited more than thirty books, including *Active Trading, Flying Blind* and *Sailing Home: A Journey*

Through Time, Place and Memory, which he describes as a floating memoir. His poetry has received a number of awards, including the Gabriela Mistral Prize from Chile, Poetry Book Society Recommendation from the U.K., the Americas Best Book Award in the 1985 Commonwealth Poetry Competition, and various prizes in Canada: the E.J. Pratt medal and prize, Archibald Lampman Prize, National Magazine Gold Award, Writers' Choice Award, and the National Poetry Prize.

Richard Harrison is the author of four books of poetry, the most recent of which, *Big Breath of a Wish*, poems about his infant daughter's development of language, recently won the W.O. Mitchell/City of Calgary Book Prize. Richard and his family have lived in Calgary since 1995 when he was Markin-Flanagan Writer-in-Residence at the University. Currently he is working on a collection of short fiction, working as a freelance editor, and teaching English at Mount Royal College.

Lala Heine-Koehn was born and educated in Poland. She studied International Law and Voice at the Handel Conservatory in Munich. She has published several collections of poetry, among them *Eyes of the Wind* (1982), *Forest Full of Rain* (1982), *The Spell of the Chaste Tree* (1994) and *The Certain Days of Abstinence*. She is also a visual artist who has exhibited her paintings in Canada and the U.S. She lives and works in Victoria, British Columbia.

Bruce Hunter was born and raised in Calgary, Alberta. He is the author of one book of short stories, *Country Music Country* (1986) and three books of poetry: *Benchmark*, (1982), *The Beekeeper's Daughter*, (1986) and *Coming Home From Home* (2000). He recently completed a novel, *Conch*, about a young deaf boy who inherits a sea shell from a great aunt which helps him "hear" into the past. His poetry and fiction draw heavily upon his Western upbringing and blue collar past. He currently teaches English at Seneca College and lives in Stratford.

Jocko's poetry has appeared in magazines in Canada, the U. S. and Australia and is the author of one poetry collection, *An Anarchist*

Dream. He is a Cape Bretoner living and sort of working in Edmonton. He is trying to get government funding to study how food deprivation makes health addicts come up with ideas like a 'fat tax.'

Since retiring from teaching, **D.G. Jones** has continued to live in North Hatley, Quebec and to publish poems and translations. Among his recent books are *Wild Asterisks in Cloud* (1997) and *Grounding Sight* (1999), both available from Empyreal Press in Montreal.

Sarah Klassen, a former teacher, is a Winnipeg poet and short fiction writer. Her most recent poetry collections are *Simone Weil: Songs of Hunger and Love* (Wolsack and Wynn, 1999) and *Dangerous Elements* (Quarry Press, 1998). She received the Gold Award for poetry in the 2001 National Magazine Awards.

Patrick Lane has published twenty-five books of poetry and fiction over the past forty years. He is widely considered to be one of the finest poets of his generation. He lives in Victoria with his companion, the poet Lorna Crozier.

Christopher Levenson was born in London, England, on February 13, 1934. He lived in the Netherlands, Germany, and the U.S.A. before moving to Ottawa in 1968. He became a citizen in 1973. He was cofounder, and for ten years editor, of *Arc* magazine, and from 1981 to 1991 founded and organized the Arc reading series in downtown Ottawa. He teaches English and Creative Writing at Carleton University and is Series Editor of Harbinger Poets, a new imprint of Carleton University Press for first books of Canadian poetry.

Jay MacPherson was born June 13, 1931 in London, England. In 1940 she moved to Newfoundland. Educated at Carleton, McGill, and University of Toronto, MacPherson taught English at University of Toronto 1957-1996. At age 18, MacPherson won the Contemporary Verse prize; in 1957 she won the Levinson prize, *Poetry* magazine. Her most well-known collection of poetry, *The Boatman* (1957), a cycle of poems examining mythic patterns of fall and redmeption, was award-ed the Governor General's award. MacPherson has also published a textbook on mythology (*Four Ages of Man: The Classical Myths*, 1962) and a study of romances (*The Spirit of Solitude: Conventions and Continuities in Late Romance*, 1982).

Performance poet **Susan McMaster** is the founding editor of *Branching Out*, a feminist quarterly. She lives in Ottawa and has performed across Canada. Her books and tapes include *Dark Galaxies* and *The Hummingbird Murders*. "Courage/Coeur de rage" is for solo performer, and uses voices and gestures—or *wordmovement*. The words to be spoken are printed in lowercase letters above each line; those to be expressed as movement are printed in capital letters below each line. Some wordmovement gestures use only one hand; use whichever hand is most comfortable. Where a body part is shown (e.g. lips or heart) the wordmovement starts there. Interpret freely.

Born in Toronto, **Colin Morton** grew up in Alberta where he completed an MA in English in 1979. He works as a teacher, editor, and writer in many media and has performed and recorded his poetry with First Draft and other music poetry groups, as well as in the animated film *Primiti Too Taa*. Also a novelist, he has been writer-in-residence at Concordia College in Minnesota (1995-96) and at Connecticut College (1997).

Poet and playwright **Daniel David Moses** is a Delaware from the Six Nations lands along the Grand River in southern Ontario. He lives in Toronto where he is a member of the Artistic Directorate of Native Earth Performing Arts. His plays include "Coyote City," "Almighty Voice and His Wife" and "The Indian Medicine Shows" which won the 1996 James Buller Memorial Award for Excellence in Aboriginal Theatre. His most recent publications include *Sixteen Jesuses* (poems, Exile Editions), *Brebeuf's Ghost* (a play, Exile Editions) and *Necropolitei* (plays, Imago). He is the co-editor of *An Anthology of Canadian Native Literature in English*.

Roger Nash was born in Maidenhead, England in 1942, and raised in Egypt and Singapore. He received a Ph.D. from the University of Exeter, and is an Associate Professor of Philosophy at Laurentian University. He is a consultant with school boards on teaching literature and art.

John Oughton has published four books of poetry between 1973 and 1997, the most recent being *Counting Out the Millennium* (Pecan Grove Press, San Antonio, TX). He has been active as a literary journalist, with about 250 articles, reviews and interviews in periodicals. Oughton studied literature at York University and at the Jack Kerouac School of Disembodied Poetics, at Naropa Institute in Boulder, Colorado. He has travelled the world, and worked at Coach House Press, and as a journalist and corporate communicator. He lives in Toronto, where he teaches community college courses and freelances as a writer and computer consultant. Currently, he is Treasurer of the League of Canadian Poets.

P.K. Page is a Companion of the Order of Canada and a life member of the League of Canadian Poets. She has published more than fifteen books of poetry, fiction and nonfiction, and has received many awards including the Oscar Blumenthal Award for Poetry (1944), the Governor General's Award for Poetry (1954), the National Magazine Award, gold (1985) and the Banff Centre of Fine Arts National Award (1989). Her most recent book is *A Kind of Fiction* (Porcupine's Quill).

Born in 1926, **James Reaney** was raised in rural Ontario and received several degrees including a PhD. from the University of Toronto, where he studied with Northrop Frye. Well-known as a dramatist for his trilogy *The Donnellys* and *Colours in the Dark* (Stratford Festival, 1967), Reaney has also published stories and poems including *Box Social, The Bully* (broadcast by the CBC) and *The Red Heart* (1950). He is married and has two children and two grandchildren.

Harold Rhenisch has published eight books of poetry, most recently *Fusion*, which provides the philosophical and lyrical underpinnings for his two previous books *Taking the Breath Away* and *The Blue Mouth of Morning*. He is also the author of the best-selling prose memoir of post-colonial orchard life in B.C.'s Similkameen Valley, *Out of the Interior: the Lost Country*. Having worked for years as a fruit-tree grafter, he currently lives on the Cariboo Plateau, where he is working on a spoof of Pound's *Cantos* and a series of poems binding native and European mythologies.

Ajmer Rode's first book, *Vishna Di Nuhar*, dealt with the theory of relativity in dialogue form inspired by Plato's *Republic*. It was published in 1966, the year he immigrated to Canada. He has published four books of poetry including *Blue Meditations* (Third Eye) and *Poems on My Doorstep* (Caitlin) in English and two others in Punjabi. He has also written and directed nine plays and is considered a founder of Canadian Punjabi threatre. He began writing full time after leaving an engineering position with BC Gas in 1994. He lives in Vancouver with his wife, Surjeet Kalsey, daughter, Surti, and son, Ankurneel.

Stan Rogal is a writer of fiction, poetry and plays. His third novel *Moon in My Pocket* will appear from Insomniac Press in the Spring of 2002, his seventh book of poems *Sub Rosa* (Wolsak and Wynn) in Spring 2003.

Linda Rogers writes to avoid the compulsion to talk. No one has timed the speed at which she does either, but it all happens fast. She and her husband Rick van Krugel sing *allegra* (Italian for fast) for short hyperactive humans. Among Linda's most recent books are *The Saning* (poetry), *The Broad Canvas* (portraits of Canadian women artists) from Sono Nis Press; and *Say My Name* (fiction) published by Ekstasis Editions in 2000.

Joe Rosenblatt was born in Toronto in 1933. He started writing seriously in the early sixties, and in 1966 his first book, *The L.S.D. Leacock*, was published by Coach House Press. Since then he has published more than a dozen books of poetry and fiction. His selected poems (1962-1975), *Top Soil*, won the Governor-General's Award for poetry. Another volume of selected poems (1963-1985), *Poetry Hotel*, won the B.C. Book Prize, 1986 for poetry. A collection of his selected drawings and new poems, *The Voluptuous Gardener*, was published last fall by Vancouver's Beach Holme Press. For the past seventeen years, Rosenblatt has been living in Qualicum Beach on Vancouver Island.

Jay Ruzesky's latest book is *Blue Himalayan Poppies* (Nightwood Editions, 2001). He lives in Victoria.

Stephen Scobie was born in Scotland on the last day of 1943, and has lived in Canada since 1965. As a poet, he has published over twenty books, and won the Governor-General's Award in 1980 for *McAlmon's Chinese Opera*. As a critic, Scobie has published extensively on Canadian literature, including studies of Sheila Watson, Leonard Cohen and bp Nichol; he has also written on topics as diverse as Cubism and Concrete Poetry, Jacques Derrida and Bob Dylan. He now teaches at the University of Victoria.

Joseph Sherman, a Maritimer, taught college English for nine years and was editor of *ARTSatlantic Magazine* for twenty-one. He lives in Prince Edward Island. A version of "Aphelion" will be included in his fifth poetry collection, *American Standard & Other Poems*, to be published in late 2001 by Oberon Press.

Born in Vancouver, **Glen Sorestad** has lived in Saskatchewan most of his life where he taught school for over twenty years. Since 1981 he has worked as a full-time writer and co-founded Thistledown Press with his wife Sonia in 1975. He has authored numerous volumes of poetry including the recent *Today I Belong to Agnes* and *Icons of Flesh* published by Ekstasis Editions. His poetry has appeared in over 30 anthologies and textbooks. Glen Sorestad lives in Saskatoon and travels widely giving readings.

Heather Spears has published eleven collections of poetry, three novels and three books of drawings. She has twice won the Pat Lowther Award and won the Governor-General's award for poetry in 1989. She has held over 75 solo exhibitions of drawings in Europe and America. Born in Vancouver, she has lived in Denmark since 1962.

Phil Thompson has been a Nova Scotian poet for more than 30 years. His own book, *All the Other Phil Thompsons are Dead* (Broken Jaw Press) has been nominated for every possible national and regional award, but short-listed for none. He seeks vengeance by writing reviews of his more successful peers. He was once drawn by Heather

Spears, and will never forget her eyes.

Poet, performer, novelist **Peter Trower** is a former logger whose collected Woods Poems, *Chainsaws in the Cathedral* (Ekstasis, 1999) featured an introduction by the late Al Purdy. Other recent publications include the poetry books *Hitting the Bricks* and *A Ship Called Destiny* (Ekstasis) and the novel *The Judas Hills* (Harbour). An exceptional poetry/jazz performer, Peter Trower lives in Gibsons, BC.

Diane L. Tucker lives in Burnaby, BC with her husband and two children. Before that she got a B.F.A. in Creative Writing from the University of BC, worked as a library clerk and had her first book of poems, *God on His Haunches*, published by Nightwood Editions (1996). When not literaturizing she may be watching *Red Dwarf*, making candles or walking the family dog, Doxa.

Phyllis Webb is well known as a poet and essayist. Her last book was *Nothing But Brush Strokes, Selected Prose,* 1995. In 1982 she received the Governor General's Award for Poetry for *The Vision Tree, Selected Poems*, published by Talon Books. She lives on Salt Spring Island where she now spends most of her time painting.

Patricia Young has published seven books of poetry, including *What I Remember From My Time on Earth,* which received the Dorothy Livesay Poetry Poetry Prize in 1998. She won a National Magazine Award for Poetry in 1999. She lives and writes in Victoria, B.C.

Terence Young's first book of poems, *The Island in Winter,* was published in the spring of 1999 by Vehicule Press. His latest book is *Rhymes With Useless.* He has won a number of awards for his fiction and poetry. He teaches at St. Michael's University School in Victoria.

Born in Virginia, **Liz Zetlin** now lives in Markdale, Ontario. Her poetry collections include *Said the River* (Penumbra Press), *Connections* (Always Press) and *The Gourd Poems,* which won the 1999 CPA Shaunt Basmajian Chapbook Award.

ACKNOWLEDGEMENTS

"Phone Lines" appears in John Barton, *Hypothesis* (House of Anansi Press, 2001).

"Notes on Mandelstam" appears in Steven Michael Berzensky, *Variations on the Birth of Jacob* (J. Gordon Shillingford Publishing, 1997).

"at waterline": Copyright 1998 Joe Blades. Published in *River Suite* by Insomniac Press and reprinted by permission.

"The lovely lines of war" appears in George Bowering, *At War With the U.S.* (Talonbooks, 1974).

from "Letter to Janey" appears in Marilyn Bowering, *Human Bodies New & Collected Poems 1987-1999* (Beachholme Publishing, 1999).

"Circular Saws" appears in Fred Cogswell, *The Long Apprenticeship* (Fiddlehead Poetry Books, 1980).

"Fovea Centralis" appears in Christopher Dewdney, *The Immaculate Perecption* (Anansi, 1986).

"Moon" appears in Richard Harrison, *Big Breath of a Wish* (Wolsak and Wynn, 1999).

"Poems for my Lovers" appears in Lala Heine-Koehn, *The Eyes of the Wind* (Turnstone Press, 1981).

"Likeness, or 'A Woman Smiling'" appears in D.G. Jones, *Grounding Sight* (Empyreal Press, 1999).

"The Line" by Daniel David Moses reprinted by permission of the author.

"Labels" appears in Ajmer Rode, *Poems At My Doorstep* (The Caitlin Press, 1990).

"Shaping" appears in Stan Rogal, *Lines of Embarkation* (Coach House Books, 1999).

"The Saning" appears in Linda Rogers, *The Saning* (Sono Nis Press, 2000).

A version of "Aphelion" appears in Joseph Sherman, *American Standard & Other Poems* (Oberon Press, 2001).

"The Teaching of Drawing" appears in Heather Spears, *Poems Selected and New* (Wolsak and Wynn, 1999).

"Hockey Poem" appears in Peter Trower, *A Ship Called Destiny: Yvonne's Book* (Ekstasis Editions, 2001).

"Walking Down the Staircase" appears in Patricia Young, *What I Remember From My Time on Earth* (House of Anansi, 1997).